Front cover illustration:
A flight of 352nd Fighter Group Mustangs escort a vee of 458th Bomb Group Liberators, both units of the 8th Air Force.

Back cover illustrations:
Top: P-51D Mustang 44-64153, VF:B, personnel 'mount' of 4th Fighter Group ace Major Fred Glover, on dispersal at Debden, Essex.
Bottom: B-17G Fortresses of 381st Bomb Group over Cambridgeshire fields, England in July 1944.

1. The first USAAF daylight bomber operation from the United Kingdom was flown on 17 August 1942 against the marshalling yards at Rouen, in France. All twelve B-17Es returned safely to Grafton Underwood. This aircraft, 41-9023, piloted by Lieutenant John Dowswell, carried VIII Bomber Command's Commanding Officer, Major General Ira Eaker, as an observer. Compared with later individual aircraft names, the inscription 'Yankee Doodle' was of modest proportions. Much of the ground equipment, like the fuel bowser, used by the pioneering 97th BG (Bomb Group) was supplied by the British.

US STRATEGIC AIRPOWER

EUROPE 1942-1945

Roger A. Freeman

ARMS AND ARMOUR

2. Lieutenant Allen Warren straps up in Spitfire V, QP:V of 2nd FS (Fighter Squadron), 52nd FG (Fighter Group) at Goxhill watched by his crew chief, Staff Sergeant Lucas. The first fighter groups to arrive in the UK were the 1st and 14th equipped with Lockheed P-38Fs and the 31st and 52nd which received Spitfires. The 31st FG saw action, but the other units had only limited operational flying before all were dispatched to North Africa to support the Allied invasion in November 1942.

▲2

3. B-17Es of the 97th BG climbing away from Grafton Underwood at 30-second intervals for the start of a

▼3

combat mission in August 1942. Up to two hours would be spent gaining an operational altitude of 20,000 feet or more, and

assembling a defensive formation before departing the English coast. In November 1942 the 97th and the second B-

17 group to become operational, the 301st, were both transferred to the North African theatre of operations.

INTRODUCTION

First published in Great Britain in
1989 by Arms and Armour Press,
Artillery House, Artillery Row,
London SW1P 1RT.

Distributed in the USA by Sterling
Publishing Co. Inc., 2 Park Avenue,
New York, NY 10016.

Distributed in Australia by
Capricorn Link (Australia) Pty. Ltd.,
P.O. Box 665, Lane Cove, New
South Wales 2066, Australia.

British Library Cataloguing in
Publication Data:
Freeman, Roger
US strategic airpower: Europe
1942–1945
1. United States Air Force. Military
aircraft, 1935–1955
I. Title.   II. Series
623.74'6'0973
ISBN 0-85368-960-1

Line artwork by Norman Ottaway.

Designed and edited by DAG
Publications Ltd. Designed by
David Gibbons; edited by Michael
Boxall; layout by Cilla Eurich;
typeset by Ronset Typesetters Ltd,
Darwen, Lancashire, and by
Typesetters (Birmingham) Limited,
Warley, West Midlands;
camerawork by M&E
Reproductions, North Fambridge,
Essex; printed and bound in Great
Britain by The Alden Press Limited,
Oxford.

Several months before the Japanese attack on Pearl Harbor and Germany's declaration of war on the United States, the US Army Air Corps had drawn up plans for the formation and commitment of a sizeable air force in a war with Nazi Germany and its allies. While ostensibly neutral, the United States had made it patently obvious where sympathy and support lay, and it was considered only a matter of time before America became involved in the European hostilities. The Army Air Corps was in the throes of becoming a semi-autonomous force whose leaders held that the complete autonomy they sought could best be achieved through establishing air power as the recognized means of achieving victory. In turn, this could best be brought about through the medium of strategic bombardment. Such a campaign, entailing the destruction of war production centres, power sources and communications, would make it extremely difficult if not impossible for an enemy to sustain a modern war. A doctrine based on this premise had long been advocated by Air Corps commanders, and was pursued with vigour once the US government was sympathetic to building offensive forces for the conflict in which it felt the nation would sooner or later become embroiled.

With agreement among the Allies to beat Nazi Germany first, the planning for a US strategic bombing force centred upon the United Kingdom as a base for operations. By the summer of 1942, when the first units were dispatched to England, a colossal force of some 2,000 heavy bombers (four-engined B-17s and B-24s) and 600 mediums (B-25s and B-26s) was proposed. The basic unit was the squadron with a complement of nine heavy bombers, a strength to be doubled when production allowed. Medium bomber squadrons initially had thirteen aircraft. However, the usual operational unit was the group, which consisted of four bomber squadrons. Each group was to occupy one airfield. The force in preparation would consist of 45 heavy and fifteen medium groups, organized into four wings – 240 squadrons. Supporting fighters were to number 800 in ten groups of three squadrons each.

The establishment of this force in the United Kingdom was never realized due to the demands of other campaigns and theatres of war. The Allied landings in North Africa late in 1942 saw the transfer and diversion of many groups in the UK. Other units raised for service in Europe were sent instead to meet emergencies in the Pacific war zones. When the Allied armies secured air bases in southern Italy, fifteen heavy bomber groups destined for England were sent to Italy to form a new strategic bombing force. Nevertheless, the heavy bomber establishment in England, designated the 8th Air Force, became – in terms of men and aircraft – the largest offensive air force of the Second World War. At peak inventory (in December 1944) it had 2,800 heavy bombers (B-17s and B-24s) and 1,400 fighters (P-47s and P-51s). Prior to this date, late in 1943, the medium bombers had been reorganized as a separate tactical force for the support of ground operations, and transferred to the 9th Air Force.

The fighter element of the 8th Air Force was developed for long-range escort of bombers and enjoyed considerable success in combating the German fighters. By the spring of 1944 VIII Fighter Command had achieved virtual mastery of the air over a large area of enemy territory. When enemy opposition in the air declined, the 8th Air

Force fighters were frequently deployed in offensive operations against enemy ground installations, notably airfields and railways.

The following photographic survey of the USAAF strategic offensive in the European Theatre of Operations (ETO) concentrates on the tool of trade, the aircraft. Additionally, through the captions, the reader is given a chronology of events, albeit simplified in the interests of brevity. The central reference section and Norman Ottaway's line-drawings round off this record of the 8th Air Force, first in a new sequence of *Warbird* titles featuring US Air Forces of the Second World War.

Roger A. Freeman

 4 ▼5

4. Bombing-up B-17E, 41-9148, 'Boomerang' with eight 500lb HE bombs. The small bomb-bay of the Fortress limited the load to 4,000 or 6,000 pounds, depending on bomb size. At the date of the photograph 'Boomerang' was serving with the 92nd BG at Bovingdon in an OTU role. Most of the 97th's B-17Es had been exchanged for B-17Fs with the 92nd before the former's departure for North Africa.

5. B-17F 41-24559, PU:C, 'Ooold Soljer', of 360th BS (Bomb Squadron) 303rd BG, taxies out at Molesworth. Externally there was little to distinguish this mark of Fortress from the B-17E apart from the one-piece moulded nose transparency. Internally there were many improvements and the B-17F equipped all new Fortress groups joining the 8th Air Force up to the autumn of 1943. The 303rd was one of four groups that provided the VIII Bomber Command B-17 strike force from November 1942 to May 1943.

6. B-17F 42-29807, WF:0, 'Lady Liberty' of the 305th BG gains flying speed as it crosses a runway intersection at Chelveston. On long-range missions these bombers were frequently filled with fuel and ordnance to near maximum overload of 72,000 pounds.

7. In wedge formations of 18 or 21 aircraft, three B-17 groups

Eight of the thirteen .50-calibre heavy guns that comprised the B-17F's defensive armament can be seen in this view. 'Lady Liberty' failed to return from a mission on 19 August 1943.

position to form a combat wing. Flying at an optimum 25,000 feet, group formations were, ideally, contained in a 1,000-foot square 'box' but there were often stragglers who, usually, through a mechanical problem, fell behind – as in this photograph.

6 ▲

7 ▼

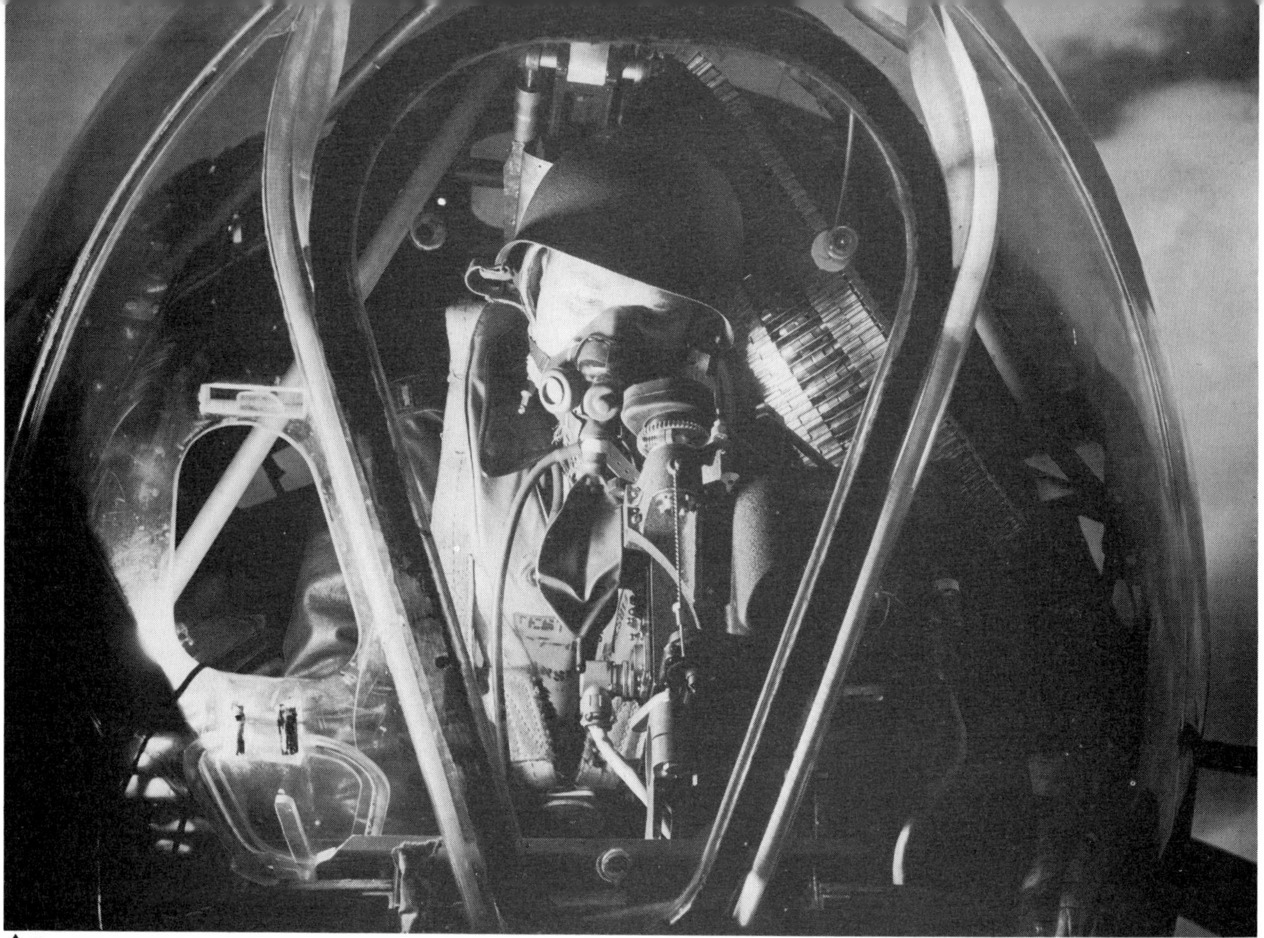

▲8

8. Accuracy in high-altitude bombing was achieved with the Norden M-7 bombsight. When given the necessary data on airspeed, drift, altitude, ballistics, etc., the instrument computed the point of bomb release and automatically dropped the bombs. This 91st BG bombardier, Lieutenant R. F. Brubaker, has an eye to the Norden telescope sighting device. He wears a standard infantry steel helmet, optional protection for crew members while in hostile airspace.

▼9

9. Two groups of Consolidated B-24D Liberators arrived in the UK during the autumn of 1942, but one, the 93rd, was soon on detached service in North Africa. The other, the 44th, initially with only three assigned squadrons instead of the normal four, suffered heavily during the winter of 1942/43. Different performance characteristics caused the B-24s to be sent in at lower altitudes and trailing the B-17s where they often attracted attention from enemy interceptors. These 44th BG B-24Ds over Norfolk in February 1943 are 41-23774, S, 'Hitler's Nightmare' and 41-23816,X, 'Black Jack' of the 68th BS, and 41-23813,L, 'Suzy Q' of 67th BS. Two were lost on operations and the other was written off before the end of 1943.

10. The strain of extreme cold and oxygen use for prolonged periods at high altitude shows on the faces of Lieutenant Harold Beasley's crew as they leave 42-5172, LL:Z, 'Thunderbird' of 401st BS, 91st BG, on 5 April 1943. At this time B-17 crews had only a one in three chance of completing a tour of 25 missions. 'Thunderbird' and the Beasley crew went down over Bremen on their next mission, twelve days later. Note that the radioman carries the gun barrel and breach removed from his machine-gun for cleaning.

11. B-17E 41-9112, 'The Dreamboat', specially modified for the 8th Air Force to feature armament improvements they desired on the Fortress. Tail turrets from B-24s were installed in nose and tail and twin .50 machine-guns located in a dorsal position. A cupola was added under the nose for the bombardier and there were several internal changes. As far as is known the aircraft was never used operationally and the changes were considered too radical to be put into production.

▲12

12. To combat growing Luftwaffe fighter opposition to the B-17 raids, 200 Republic P-47C Thunderbolts were sent to the UK early in 1943 to equip the 4th, 56th and 78th FGs. These, being put through their paces over King's Cliffe, were flown by 56th FG pilots, the unit which had service tested the type in the USA. In the foreground is 'Invasion II' of 401st BS, 91st BG, a B-17F lost a few weeks later on 17 April 1943.

13. P-47Cs and Ds of 83rd FS, 78th FG, over East Anglia on a fine spring day in 1943. The Thunderbolt was both large and heavy in comparison with its British and German contemporaries and had a poor rate of climb. In the rarified air above 20,000 feet, however, its performance improved dramatically through effective turbo-supercharging of its powerful engine.

▼13

14. An experimental venture, the YB-40 was a B-17F fitted with a Bendix 'chin' turret, an additional power turret in the radio room and twin guns in each waist position. Carrying no bombs, it was intended that the aircraft should perform a defensive role on the extremities of B-17 formations. In practice it was found to have undesirable flying characteristics due to the extra weight aft, and to be equally as vulnerable as the B-17Fs it was supposedly protecting. The 327th BS, 92nd BG operated twelve of these aircraft for a short period during the summer of 1943. This YB-40 is 42-5736, UX:C.

15. 'Kipling's Error III', 42-5885, of 413th BS, 96th BS flies through 88mm Flak bursts while on its bomb run. The 96th was one of the 'new' B-17 groups entering the action in the spring of 1943. In May and June VIII Bomber Command's force was trebled and by early August sixteen B-17 groups were penetrating deep into Germany to strike strategic targets. The force was composed of two wings, the 1st, identified by a triangle marking on tail fins, and the 4th, which used a square device. A letter within the symbol identified the group in the wing. Later in the year these two wings were redesignated as divisions but retained the same markings.

16 17

16. To an untrained observer a heavy bomber formation appeared to have no order. In fact each was made up of three-plane vees, echeloned up and down to uncover as many defensive guns as possible. A close formation also provided a good bomb pattern. Here 385th BG B-17Fs head for a target. Nearest the camera is 42-30264,S, 'Dorsal Queen'.

17. The Thunderbolt could only penetrate a few miles beyond the coast of continental Europe until equipped with external disposable fuel tanks. Paper-plastic ferry tanks were first tried, but fuel could not be drawn from these at high altitude due to lack of pressurization. They did, however, enable P-47s to reach the Netherlands/Germany border on a few occasions in the high summer of 1943. One of these 'bathtub' tanks is fitted to Lieutenant Colonel James Stone's personal P-47C, 41-6373, HL:Z seen at Duxford during an engine run-up. The wooden wedge helped force tank clear of aircraft when released.

18▲   19▼

18. Crossing the Alps; B-17F 42-30601,K of 548th BS, 385th BG. On 17 August 1943, a year after VIII Bomber Command's initial heavy bomber operation, an audacious raid was made on the Schweinfurt ball-bearing works and the Messerschmitt fighter plant at Regensburg. Instead of returning to England the Regensburg force turned south across Italy and made for bases in North Africa. A few days later it 'shuttled' across France back to England.

20▼

19 & 20. Messerschmitt Bf 109-Gs diving to attack B-17s of the 95th BG over Bremen and a Focke-Wulf Fw 190A coming in to fire at 305th BG Fortresses over the same target. Luftwaffe fighter opposition had increased to a point where on many unescorted, deep-penetration missions the VIII Bomber Command was incurring near prohibitive losses during the late summer and early autumn of 1943.

▲21
21. 'Rodger the Lodger II', 42-30377 R of 412th BS, 95th BG in its death throes. Flames trail from the wing behind No. 2 engine with feathered prop. Shortly after this photograph was taken the fuel fumes in a

▼22

wing tank exploded and the wing failed. All the crew perished; the only fatalities on a very successful mission to the Marienburg aircraft factory.

22. 'Cabin In The Sky', 42-30338, FC:P of 571st BS, 390th BG. On 10 October 1943 the gunners on this aircraft were credited with destroying eleven enemy fighters on a mission to Münster. While this was an exaggerated figure due to the

problem of several gunners shooting at the same enemy fighter and all claiming its destruction, it was, nevertheless, indicative of the intensity of the air battle.

23. B-17Fs of the 305th Bomb Group turn over burning Schweinfurt, 14 October 1943. On this occasion VIII Bomber Command took its heaviest loss to date against a single target; sixty B-17s. A sobering lesson that these unescorted raids were too costly to sustain.

24. Despite the Thunderbolt's shortcomings, many US pilots were learning to use the fighter to advantage. With sufficient altitude they could dive on enemy aircraft preparing to attack the bombers and successfully shoot them down. First US fighter ace – five or more aerial victories – was Captain Charles London (right) and the second, Major Eugene Roberts (in cockpit). Both served with the 78th FG at Duxford.

23▲   24▼

Major E.P. ROBERTS
T/Sgt N.H SAPPER
Chief

25. In August 1943 the 56th FG at Halesworth commenced a succession of spectacular successes which took it far ahead of all other fighter groups in numbers of enemy aircraft shot down. Their first ace was Captain Gerald Johnson who flew P-47D 42-7977, HV:D, 'In The Mood', seen here with one of the metal pressurized 'drop tanks' which enabled P-47s to fly as far as Emden and the Ruhr on escort missions.

26. General 'Hap' Arnold, Chief of the US Air Forces, talks to Brigadier General Curtis LeMay during a visit to the 8th Air Force, autumn 1943. Arnold was being shown a battle-damaged B-17F of 379th BG which force-landed at Bury St Edmunds. Back to camera is Brigadier General Fred Anderson of VIII Bomber Command.

27. A number of celebrities served with the 8th Army Air Force including film star Clark Gable who flew five missions while making a film on air gunners and air gunnery. Gabl

28 ▲

served in B-17s; another famous Hollywood actor, James Stewart, was a squadron commander in a B-24 group.

28. In the final months of 1943 much effort was expended on giving escort fighters additional range. The British-made paper/plastic 108 US gallon drop tank extended the Thunderbolts' radius of action to 325 miles from base. These silver-coloured tanks are carried on the belly shackles of 78th FG P-47Ds marshalling on the PSP (Pierced Steel Plank) runway at Duxford.

29. Lieutenant Thwaite taxies P-47D 42-75214, QI:L at Martlesham Heath, an aircraft of one of the new Thunderbolt groups that arrived in the UK during the autumn of 1943. By the end of the year VIII Fighter Command had nine P-47 groups on strength.

30. Unmistakable shape in the English sky: P-38H Lightnings of the 20th FG 'peel off' over King's Cliffe. After an absence of a year, Lightnings were again operational with VIII Fighter Command. Unfortunately, the Allison power plants suffered from low temperature problems which led to many failures. This and other operational difficulties with the P-38 limited the aircraft's usefulness.

29 ▼

30 ▼

▲31

31. Work on a P-38H of 55th FG at Nuthampstead. Despite its problems, the P-38 was able to extend the radius of escort for bombers to between 400 and 500 miles from base. These 150 US gallon capacity drop tanks, carried one under each inboard wing section, were the means of providing this range.

32. Lieutenant Colonel Jack
▼32
Jenkins, 55th FG CO's P-38H, 42-67074, 'Texas Ranger' on dispersal at Nuthampstead, October 1943. In 'Texas Ranger IV' Jenkins led the first US fighters over Berlin on 3 March 1944.

33. The fighter which gave the 8th Air Force the long-range fighter capability it sought was the North American P-51B Mustang. The P-51B had a radius of action of 400 miles on its internal fuel supply alone; with two 75 US gallon drop tanks this was pushed out to more than 600 miles. 'Peg O' My Heart', 43-12173, GQ:A served with the 355th FS, 354th FG at Boxted, the first base to receive the Merlin-engined Mustang. Although assigned to the 9th Air Force for tactical operations, the 354th FG spent its first four months under VIII Fighter Command control, flying mostly as bomber escorts.

34. Mustangs of the 354th FG fly over a new B-17G, 42-37773, T, 'Full House' of the 561st BS, 388th BG during the Bremen mission of 22 December 1943. This Fortress failed to return from its next mission two days later.

33▲ 34▼

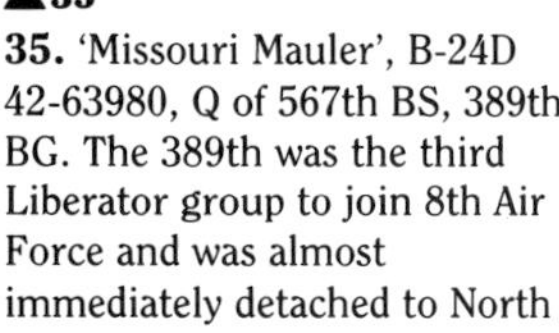

35. 'Missouri Mauler', B-24D 42-63980, Q of 567th BS, 389th BG. The 389th was the third Liberator group to join 8th Air Force and was almost immediately detached to North

▼36

Africa. In October 1943 the B-24 force was finally re-established in England and began to expand rapidly. Only the 44th, 93rd and 389th BGs operated B-24Ds on bombing operations. Note single

.50 machine-gun through rear under hatch, one in each waist window and two in the nose.

36. Gear down, B-24H, 42-7585, RN:A of 703rd BS, 445th

BG about to turn in on final approach to Tibenham. The 445th was one of four new Liberator groups that commenced operations before the end of 1943. With better defensive armament, including a nose turret, the B-24H was much heavier than the D model and required careful handling with a full war load. Most early B-24Hs came from the giant Ford plant at Willow Run, Michigan.

37. B-17Gs 42-31447, BX:D, 'Cookie' and 42-31718, AW:T of 338th and 337th BSs, 96th BG en route to a target. The first B-17Gs reached the squadrons late in September 1943 and by the end of the year the G had become the predominant model. The Bendix 'chin turret', first seen on the YB-40, was the feature that distinguished the G from the F. However, from a pilot's standpoint the introduction of electronic in place of hydraulic operated turbo-superchargers was the major improvement giving easier and less troublesome control.

231718
T
231447
C
D
BX

38. On short-haul missions the B-17's load could be increased by the installation of underwing racks. These 385th BG armourers are securing a 1,000lb HE bomb. The racks were little used because they severely impaired range and performance.

39. B-24J 42-100347,*M* of 705th BS, 446th BG unloads 500lb HE bombs from 17,000 feet over an aircraft plant at Gotha on 20 February 1944. The mission was one of a series flown against the German aircraft industry during a period known as 'Big Week'. Note the guns of the retracted ball turret projecting below the fuselage of this Liberator. As the turret adversely affected flying stability it was removed from most B-24s during the spring of 1944.

▲38　▼39

40. A contrailing 306th BG B-17 salvoes eight 500-pounders over Berlin. Early in March the 8th Air Force carried out its first attacks on the German capital. The battle on the 6th reached epic proportions with the loss of 69 heavies and eleven fighters. German losses were some 90 aircraft.

41. After suffering engine failure during the 8th Air Force's first major attack on Berlin, B-24H 41-29191 'Hello Natural' of 712th BS, 448th BG sought sanctuary in Sweden. More than 140 USAAF bombers and fighters crashed or force-landed in neutral Sweden during hostilities when damage or mechanical difficulties made safe return to the UK unlikely after a mission deep into northern Germany. Switzerland served as a similar refuge in the south.

▲42

42. Armourers about to load a 500lb bomb on the 'belly' shackles of 'Sis', 42-8602, YJ:E of 351st FS at Metfield. Although the primary duty of 8th Air Force fighter groups was the support of heavy bombers, during the winter of 1943-44 an offensive role was developed for fighter units to take advantage of those days when they were not required as escorts. Enemy airfields and communications were the usual targets for fighter-bombing.

43. The P-47 had a reputation for looking after its pilot. When Lieutenant Comstock was forced to 'belly in' near Lowestoft on 3 February 1944 he was able to walk away from the wreck of his aircraft. The engine cut out because of fuel shortage after return from a long mission where the 56th FG had been heavily engaged in combats.

▼43

US 8TH AIR FORCE ORDER OF BATTLE: JUNE 1944

1ST BOMB DIVISION

1st Bomb Wing B-17

91ST BG	322, 323, 324, 401 BS	Bassingbourn
381ST BG	532, 533, 534, 535 BS	Ridgewell
398TH BG	600, 601, 602, 603 BS	Nuthampstead

40th Bomb Wing B-17

92ND BG	325, 326, 327, 407 BS	Podington
305TH BG	364, 365, 366, 422 BS	Chelveston
306TH BG	367, 368, 369, 423 BS	Thurleigh

41st Bomb Wing B-17

303RD BG	358, 359, 360, 427 BS	Molesworth
379TH BG	524, 525, 526, 527 BS	Kimbolton
384TH BG	544, 545, 546, 547 BS	Grafton Underwood

94th Bomb Wing B–17

351ST BG	508, 509, 510, 511 BS	Polebrook
401ST BG	612, 613, 614, 615 BS	Deenethorpe
457TH BG	748, 749, 750, 751 BS	Glatton

2ND BOMB DIVISION

2nd Bomb Wing B-24

389TH BG	564, 565, 566, 567 BS	Hethel
445TH BG	700, 701, 702, 703 BS	Tibenham
453RD BG	732, 733, 734, 735 BS	Old Buckenham

14th Bomb Wing B-24

44TH BG	66, 67, 68, 506 BS	Shipdham
392ND BG	576, 577, 578, 579 BS	Wendling
492ND BG	856, 857, 858, 859 BS	North Pickenham

20th Bomb Wing B-24

93RD BG	328, 329, 340, 409 BS	Hardwick
446TH BG	704, 705, 706, 707 BS	Bungay
448TH BG	712, 713, 714, 715 BS	Seething

95th Bomb Wing B-24

489TH BG	844, 845, 846, 847 BS	Halesworth
491ST BG	852, 853, 854, 855 BS	Metfield

96th Bomb Wing B-24

458TH BG	752, 753, 754, 755 BS	Horsham St. Faith
466TH BG	784, 785, 786, 787 BS	Attlebridge
467TH BG	789, 790, 791 BS	Rackheath

3RD BOMB DIVISION

4th Bomb Wing B-17

94TH BG	331, 332, 333, 410 BS	Bury St. Edmunds
385TH BG	548, 549, 550, 551 BS	Great Ashfield
447TH BG	708, 709, 710, 711 BS	Rattlesden

13th Bomb Wing B-17

95TH BG	334, 335, 336, 412 BS	Horham
100TH BG	349, 350, 351, 418 BS	Thorpe Abbotts
390TH BG	568, 569, 570, 571 BS	Framlingham

45th Bomb Wing B-17

96TH BG	337, 338, 339, 413 BS	Snetterton Heath
388TH BG	560, 561, 562, 563 BS	Knettishall
452ND BG	728, 729, 730, 731 BS	Deopham Green

92nd Bomb Wing B-24

486TH BG	832, 833, 834, 835 BS	Sudbury
487TH BG	836, 837, 838, 839 BG	Lavenham

93rd Bomb Wing B-24

34TH BG	4, 7, 18, 391 BS	Mendlesham
490TH BG	848, 849, 851 BS	Eye
493RD BG	860, 861, 862, 863 BS	Debach

VIII FIGHTER COMMAND

65th Fighter Wing

4TH FG	334, 335, 336 FS	P-51	Debden
56TH FG	61, 62, 63 FS	P-47	Boxted
355TH FG	354, 357, 358 FS	P-51	Steeple Morden
356TH FG	359, 360, 361 FS	P-47	Martlesham
479TH FG	434, 435, 436 FS	P-38	Wattisham
	5 ERS	P-47	Boxted

66th Fighter Wing

55TH FG	38, 338, 343 FS	P-38	Wormingford
78TH FG	82, 83, 84 FS	P-47	Duxford
339TH FG	503, 504, 505 FS	P-51	Fowlmere
353RD FG	350, 351, 352 FS	P-47	Raydon
357TH FG	362, 363, 364 FS	P-51	Leiston

67th Fighter Wing

20TH FG	55, 77, 79 FS	P-38	King's Cliffe
352ND FG	328, 486, 487 FS	P-51	Bodney
359TH FG	368, 369, 370 FS	P-51	East Wretham
361ST FG	374, 375, 376 FS	P-51	Bottisham
364TH FG	383, 384, 385 FS	P-38	Honington

VIII COMPOSITE COMMAND

801ST BG(P)	36, 406, 788, 850 BS	B-24	Harrington
495TH FTG	551, 552 FS	P-47	Atcham
496TH FTG	554, 555 FS	P-38 & P-51	Goxhill
803 BS(P)		B-17	Oulton

Under 8AF HQ

7PG	13, 14, 22, 27 PS	Spitfire & F-5	Mount Farm
802 RG(P)	652, 653, 654, BS(P)	B-24 & Mosquito	Watton

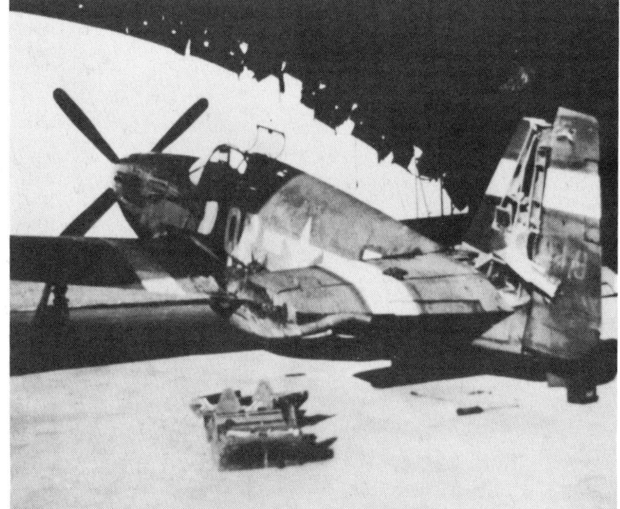

44. In an air fight over south-west France, Captain Duane Beeson shot down an enemy fighter but took a shell in the tail of his P-51B 43-6819, QP:B. Beeson was to become one of the leading Mustang aces in the 4th FG, the first 8th Air Force unit to convert from P-47s to P-51s, a programme which began in February 1944. (F. Bodner)

BOEING B-17G-65-DL FORTRESS 44-6801

of 412th Bomb Squadron, 95th Bomb
Group, based at Horham, Suffolk, April 1945

Wingspan 103ft 9in
Length 74ft 4in
Empty weight 36,135lb
Max. loaded weight 72,000lb
Power plant (×4) Wright R-1820-97
1,200hp radial
Max. speed 287mph at 25,000ft
Operational cruise speed 195mph
Best rate of climb 37 minutes
to 20,000ft
Normal range 2,000 miles
Normal bomb load 4,000lb
Max. bomb load 13,600lb
Armament twelve .50in MG
Crew 9 or 10

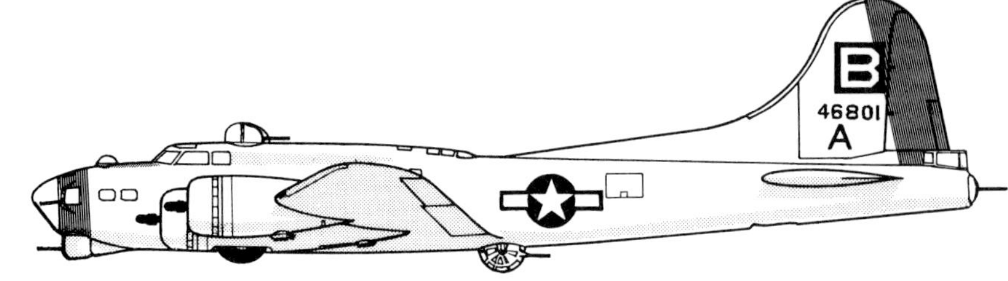

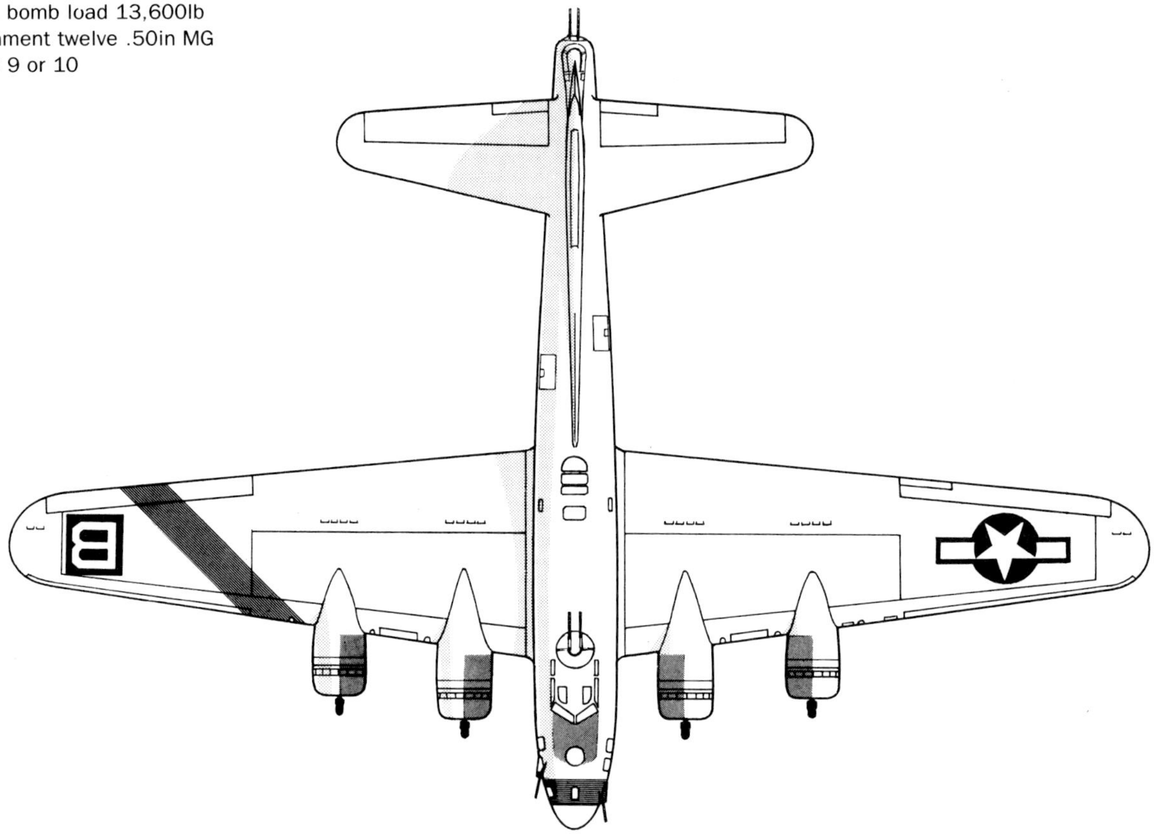

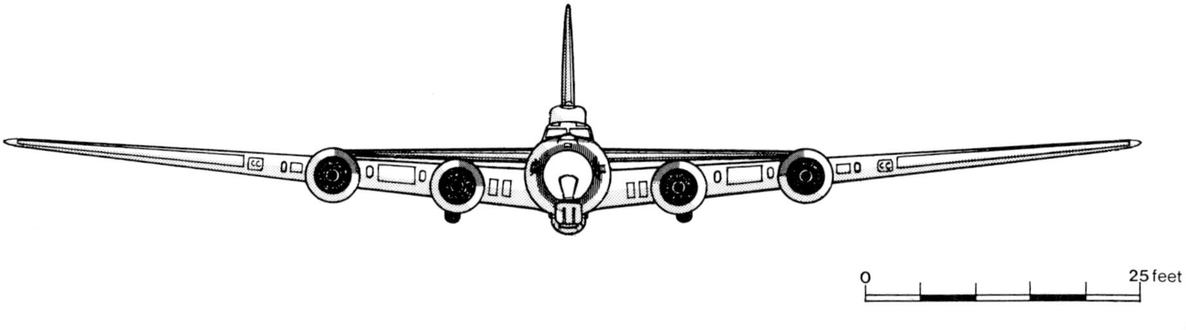

CONSOLIDATED B-24J-155-CO 44-40275

of 753rd Bomb Squadron, 458th Bomb Group,
based at Horsham St. Faith, Norfolk, October 1944

Wingspan 110ft
Length 67ft 2in
Empty weight 36,500lb
Max. loaded weight 67,800lb
Power plant (×4) Pratt & Whitney R-1830-65
1,200hp radial
Max. speed 290mph
Operational cruise speed 205mph
Best rate of climb 25 minutes
to 20,000ft
Normal range 2,100 miles
Normal bomb load 5,000lb
Max. bomb load 12,800lb
Armament ten .50in MG
Crew 9 or 10

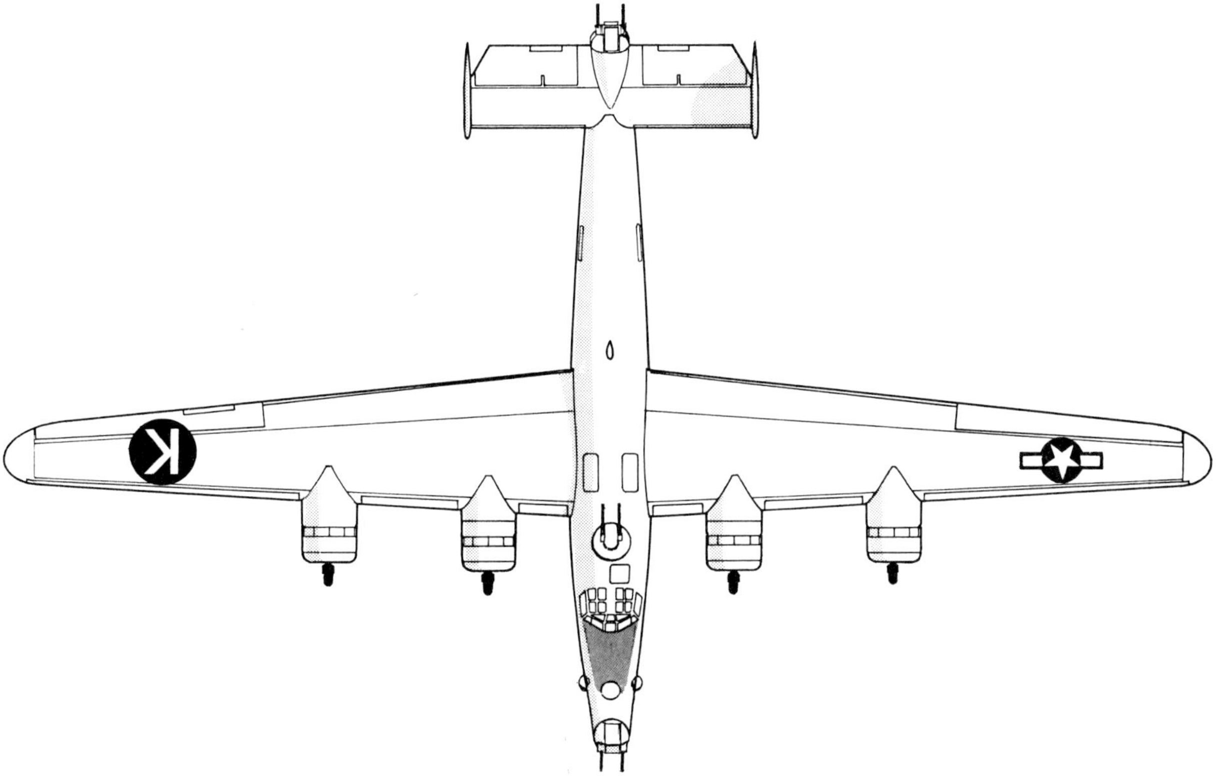

US STRATEGIC AIRPOWER: EUROPE 1942–1945

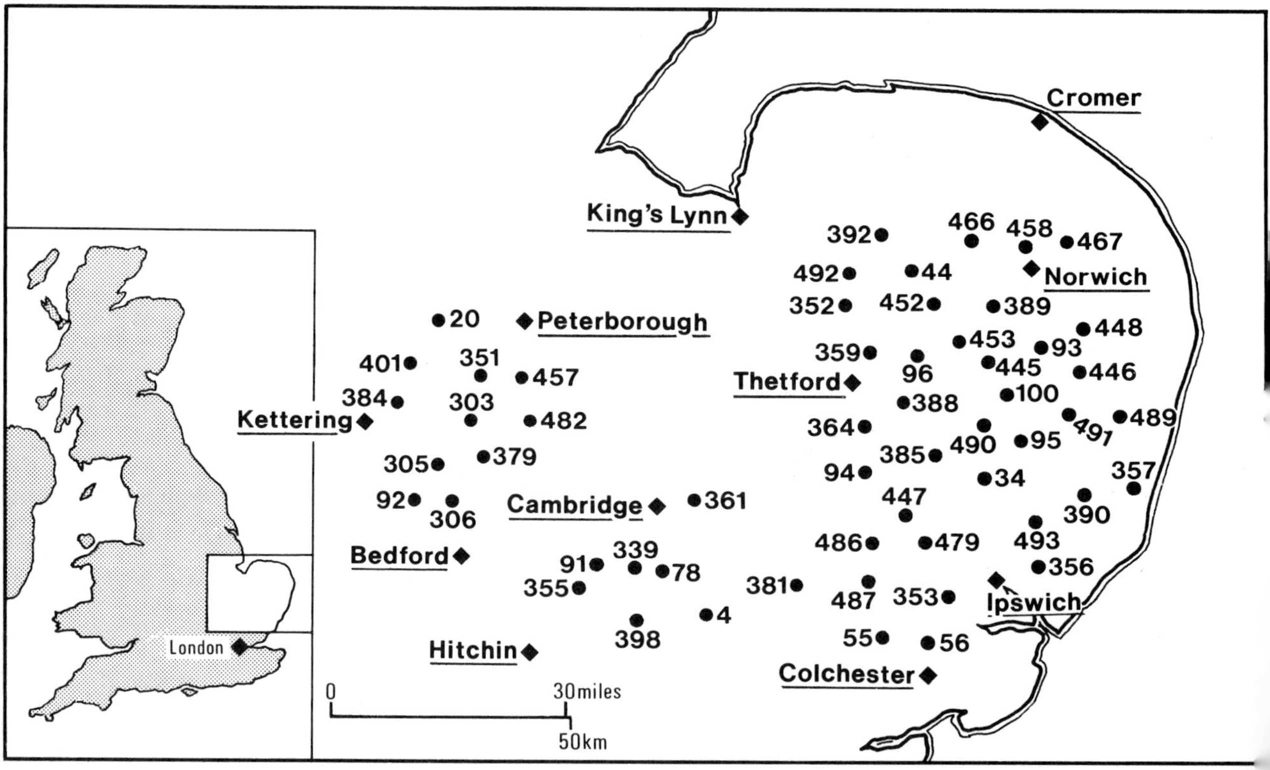

45. From February 1944, escort fighters were permitted to drop down to low level and strafe. Here a 78th FG P-47 peppers a water tower suspected of housing light Flak.

45 ▲

46 ▲

46. Flying-boats of a Luftwaffe training unit were shot up on a lake near Lyons by Mustangs of the 4th FG on the last day of April 1944. From the early spring of 1944 no Luftwaffe air base in western Europe was safe from US fighters and several massed strafing raids on airfields were carried out.

47. P-47 pilots Captain Charles Dinse and Lieutenant Richard Stearns of 353rd FG dispatched this Bf 110 over Germany on 24 January 1944. The white paintwork suggests that the Messerschmitt had recently been transferred from the Eastern Front.

47 ▼

▲48

48. Another 4th FG pilot who had considerable success flying Mustangs in the spring of 1944 was Captain Done Gentile, an ex-RAF Eagle Squadron pilot. His colourful P-51B, 43-6913, VF:T had a personal identity display of red-and-white checkers. In this picture Gentile had just returned to Debden from a mission. (G. Weckbacker)

49. Following the Bodney-based 352nd FG's conversion from P-47s to P-51s, its squadrons had several successful air battles over Germany. Here commander of 487th FS, Major John Meyer (third from left) poses with other pilots after the mission of 8 May 1944 when the group claimed 24 victories.

▼49

50. Captain Maurice McClary taxies out at King's Cliffe in 'Murph III', P-38J, 42-69131, KI:J. By the early spring of 1944 many replacement aircraft arriving in the UK were in natural metal finish. At this time it was USAAF policy to discontinue camouflage paint on all aircraft except for special requirements such as night fighters.

51. As an inducement to US citizens to invest in war bonds, aircraft could be 'bought' through special savings drives. The organization which subscribed the required sum was acknowledged with a suitable inscription on a production aircraft. Lieutenant Donald Corrigan and ground crew pose with one such aircraft operated by 352nd FS. The photograph was to be conveyed to the Republic factory to show employees that their investment was helping to win the war.

52. Captain Robert S. Johnson is carried shoulder-high by fellow pilots of the 56th FG after destroying his 27th and 28th enemy aircraft on 8 May 1944. Johnson's total was then the highest of any US pilot flying in Europe, but the figure was equalled in July by Lieutenant Colonel Francis Gabreski, seen at the left in this picture. The P-47D in the background on the Boxted hardstand is Gabreski's HV:A.

53. A 490th BG B-24H crossing the threshold of Eye airfield in the Suffolk farmlands. The 490th was one of five B-24 Liberator groups assigned to the 3rd Bomb Division in April and May 1944 to give this organization a mixed force of B-17s and B-24s. All the B-24 groups were eventually converted to B-17s to improve operational efficiency.

▲52 ▼53

54. Resplendent in black-and-white 'D-Day' markings, a Spitfire XI, PL 767, at Mount Farm in early June 1944. The 14th PS (Photographic Squadron) operated a dozen of these aircraft for long-range, high-altitude photography of strategic targets. This particular aircraft crashed on return from operations later the same month. (P. Piscitelli)

55. Principal type used by the 7th PG (Photographic Group) in support of 8th Air Force operations was the camera-carrying version of the P-38 designated F-5. Cameras were housed in the nose compartment in lieu of armament. F-5E 'Sis and Willie' has an oblique-facing camera port on the left side.

▲56

56. The 25th BG(R) at Watton operated two squadrons of Mosquito XVIs for night photography and weather reconnaissance. Because of its high speed the type was also popular for specialized scouting missions, dispensing 'chaff' (anti-radar foil) in front of heavy bomber formations.

57. By D-Day, 6 June 1944, only four P-47 groups remained in VIII Fighter Command. While the primary mission continued to be bomber support, escort duties were usually assigned to P-51s, and the P-47 units were given ground attack missions. The P-47 Thunderbolt could deliver a hefty punch as this P-47D-25 (42-26357, LH:V) shows. Three 4.5in rocket tubes and 250lb bombs under each wing plus a 150 US gallon capacity drop tank under the fuselage make up the load. Note 'bubble' canopy of this P-27D-25 Mk RE.

58. The 'bubble' cockpit canopy was also a feature of the new Mustangs arriving from June 1944 onwards. The pilot was given excellent all-round visibility, but the cut-down rear fuselage adversely affected directional control. This P-51D, cavorting over the patchwork fields of Suffolk, was the personal 'mount' of 357th FG's Donald Bochkay.

57▲   58▼

▲59

59. Royal visit. King George VI and Queen Elizabeth meet the ground crew of 379th BG's 'Four Of A Kind', 43-37777, at Kimbolton in July 1944. Lieutenant General James

▼60

Doolittle, Commander of 8th Air Force, is their escort, while Princess Elizabeth talks to another US officer. Aircraft nickname was derived from the last four digits of the serial number.

60. By the early summer of 1944 enemy fighter opposition was no longer the threat it had been to the US strategic

bombing campaign, such was the attrition suffered by the Luftwaffe in aircraft and pilots during the spring. Anti-aircraft artillery defences, however, claimed an increasing number of B-17s and B-24s during the following months. Here a B-17 goes down in flames after taking an 88mm Flak hit over an oil target at Ruhland in Germany.

61. Despite this gaping wound made by an exploding 105mm shell, B-17G 42-98004, YB:H of 508th BS, 351st BG, was brought back to base at Polebrook. The Flak hit was sustained while bombing near Cologne and both radio operator and ball turret gunner were killed. The damage says much for the sound construction of the Fortress.

62. 'Hitler's Headache', B-17G 42-97321, KY:A taxies to its dispersal while a squadron of Fortresses prepares to break formation and land at Chelveston after a mission. The inner engines were stopped after landing as this improved manoeuvring on the ground.

61▲   62▼

63. Men of the 357th FG pose with Russian airmen in front of a PE-2 at Piryatin, Russia. On three occasions during the second half of 1944 a force of 8th Air Force B-17s, and part of their P-51 escorts, continued to land at Russian bases after attacking targets in north-east Germany or Poland. From the USSR the force flew to Italy, attacking targets on the way, and finally the third leg of the shuttle took them home to the UK. (via M. Olmsted)

64. Lieutenant Charles 'Chuck' Yeager of 357th FG about to climb into his Mustang at Leiston. On 12 October 1944 he shot down five enemy aircraft during a single escort mission, a feat achieved by several other US pilots in the last year of hostilities. Apart from being an indication of personal prowess, such events also illustrated the poor calibre of most new Luftwaffe pilots and their inadequate training.

65. A close formation of 467th BG Liberators bomb on smoke markers released by their Pathfinder leadship, B-24L, 44-50151, 4Z:T–, equipped with H2S ground-scanning radar. From the spring of 1944 such Pathfinders flew in all large formations to enable bombing to take place if cloud obscured the target.

66. The strike camera which operated automatically when bombs were released caught the death throes of a 458th BG B-24 which took a direct Flak hit over Hamm on 12 December 1944.

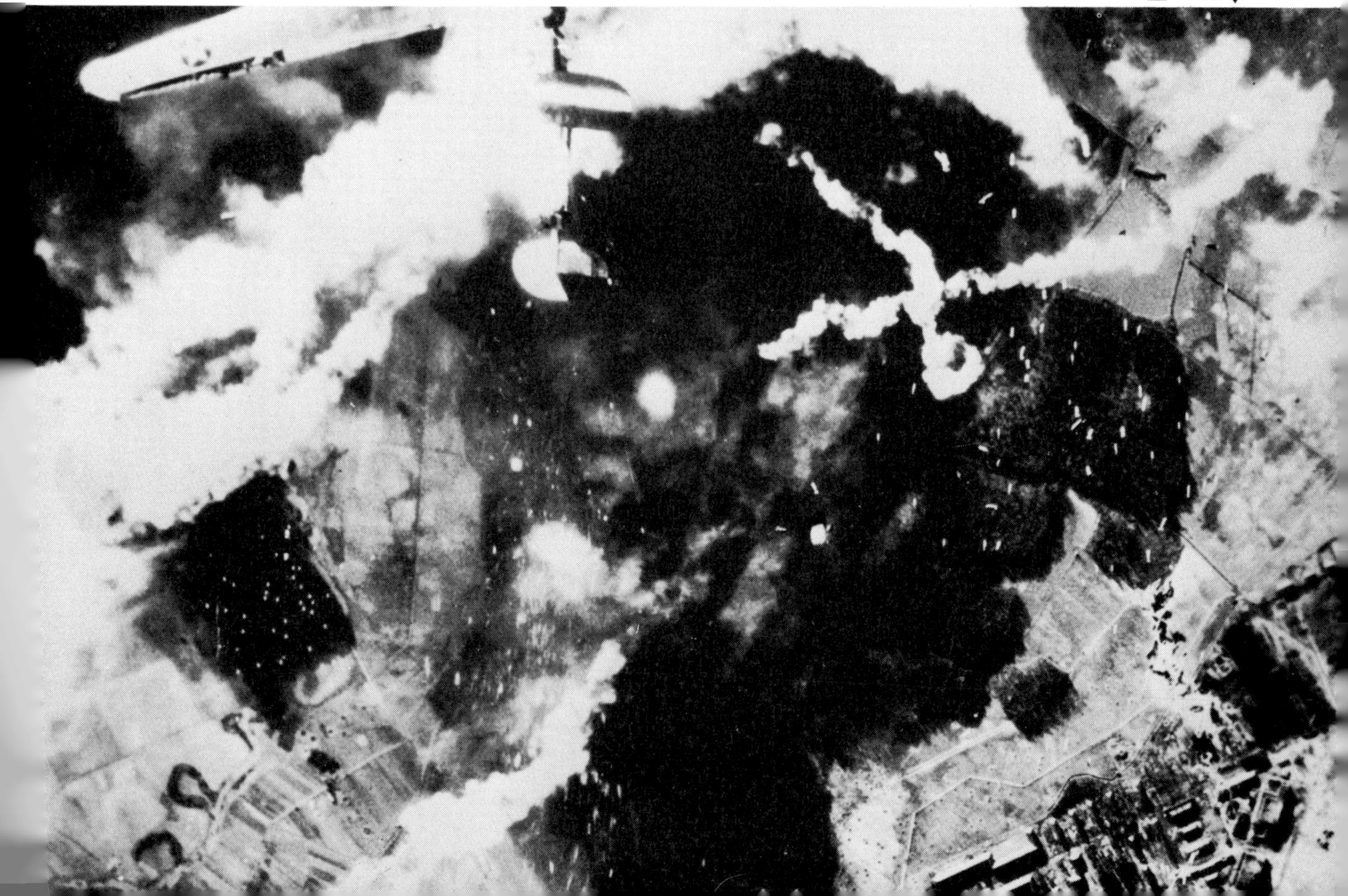

▲ 67

67. The winter of 1944/45 was severe by UK standards with long periods of snow and freezing fog. Weather caused many diversions. This B-24J of 701st BS, 445th BG sits in the snow at Framlingham until visibility improves.

68. On New Year's Day 1945 the Luftwaffe made a last major attack on Allied airfields in liberated Belgium and France. Many 8th Air Force aircraft that had been diverted for repair or refuelling were destroyed by strafing. B-24H 41-28962, Q2:S of 790th BS, 467th BG being one bomber that was hit and burnt out. (R. Zorn)

69. Wing fires were the cause of loss of a large number of B-17s and B-24s. Fumes in empty tanks would explode on ignition, often leading to failure of the wing at that section. There were, however, many lucky escapes, such as that of B-17G 43-38633 which had a main fuel cell ignite and burn away a large part of the wing's trailing edge. The 379th BG pilot, Lieutenant Newton Kerr, was able to fly the aircraft back to Woodbridge, having regained control after ordering his crew to bale out over the continent.

70. Clutching two 108 US gallon 'paper' tanks, an element of 79th FS, 20th FG P-51Ds head out on another mission over Germany. The appearance of German jet and rocket-propelled fighters during the final months of hostilities posed a new threat to the US 8th Air Force heavy bombers. Despite the jets being some 100mph faster than the US escort fighters, P-51 Mustangs continued to dominate the skies over the enemy homeland and were able to shoot down several Me 262s, the principal jet antagonists.

▼ 68

▲71

71. By January 1945 all but one of 8th Air Force's fifteen fighter groups had converted to Mustangs, the last being the 78th FG at Duxford. Lieutenant Colonel John Landers, the CO, flew this highly decorated Mustang. The P-51 exhibited at the Imperial War Museum in London has been painted to represent this aircraft.

72. Late in 1944 each fighter group was expanded to include its own Operational Training Unit. New pilots received training in the group's operational procedures and the flying control system used in Europe before commencing combat missions. Well-worn fighters – indicated by the WW (War Weary) marking – were used for these purposes and sometimes showed their age. The demise of 55th FG's 43-12438, one of the first P-51Bs to reach the UK and serve with 354th FG, was due to engine failure.

▼72

73. The only fighter group retaining the Thunderbolt was the 56th FG which began to receive the P-47M model early in 1945. Basically, the new model was a P-47D airframe with a more powerful engine, the 'C' type version of the Pratt & Whitney 2800. Despite difficulties with this new power plant, the P-47M proved to have a top speed in excess of the P-51s at high altitudes. The 56th FG ended the war as the top-scoring 8th Air Force fighter group in Europe in the numbers of enemy aircraft shot down.

74. The heavy bomber loss rate, as a percentage of sorties flown, fell dramatically during the final weeks of 8th Army Air Force operations. As a result individual aircraft survived to complete large totals of missions, in some cases in excess of 100. The champion Liberator was B-24H 'Witchcraft', 42-52534, Q2:*M* of 790th BS, 467th BG, which had 130 missions completed with no turnbacks due to mechanical or equipment failure. 'Witchcraft' was also one of the few original B-24s with which the 467th began operations in April 1944.

73 ▲

74 ▼

▲75 ▼76

75. & 76. The highest total of missions completed by a B-17 without having suffered a mechanical turnback was the 140 achieved by the 323rd BS, 91st BG's 'Nine O Nine', 42-31909, OR:R. A B-17G, of 379th BG flew 157 missions, but this aircraft had 'aborted' on two occasions. Compare the photograph of 'Nine O Nine' taken in April 1945 with that of 'Delta Rebel No 2', a B-17F of the same unit photographed on the same hardstand at Bassingbourn in April 1943. 'Delta Rebel No 2', 42-5077, OR:T, was one of the first Fortresses in the 8th Air Force to complete 25 missions, but was lost on the first Schweinfurt mission, 17 August 1943. In the foreground is Lieutenant Charles 'Red' Cliburn, the bomber's usual pilot in April 1943.

77. Some very colourful markings appeared on 8th Air Force aircraft in the spring of 1945, particularly the liaison types. Typical is the brush and spraywork which turned this Piper L-4 into a ferocious beast.

78. Collisions in the crowded sky over East Anglia had been a not infrequent occurrence throughout the 8th Air Force's near 1000-day campaign, and continued to be in the immediate post-war days. A few weeks after VE-Day two 96th BG Fortresses collided over Norfolk. The pilot of 44-8451, AW:D managed to crash-land but the aircraft was consumed by fire.

▲79

79, 80, 81, 82, 83 & 84. US bombers were well known for their 'nose art' and this was so for the majority of 8th Air Force B-17s and B-24s. Pin-up girls were the most popular subject of which the examples here show: 'Just Once More', 44-8854 of 94th BG; 'Pugnacious Princess Pat', 44-10579 of 389th BG; 'Paper Doll' 42-3492 of 482nd BG; and 'Just Plain Lonesome', 42-39975 of 91st BG. Frivolous was 'Biff Bam', 42-95283 of 466th BG, while a patriotic stance was taken with 'Winnie, Frank and Joe', 42-97954 of 91st BG.

80▶

▼81

▼82

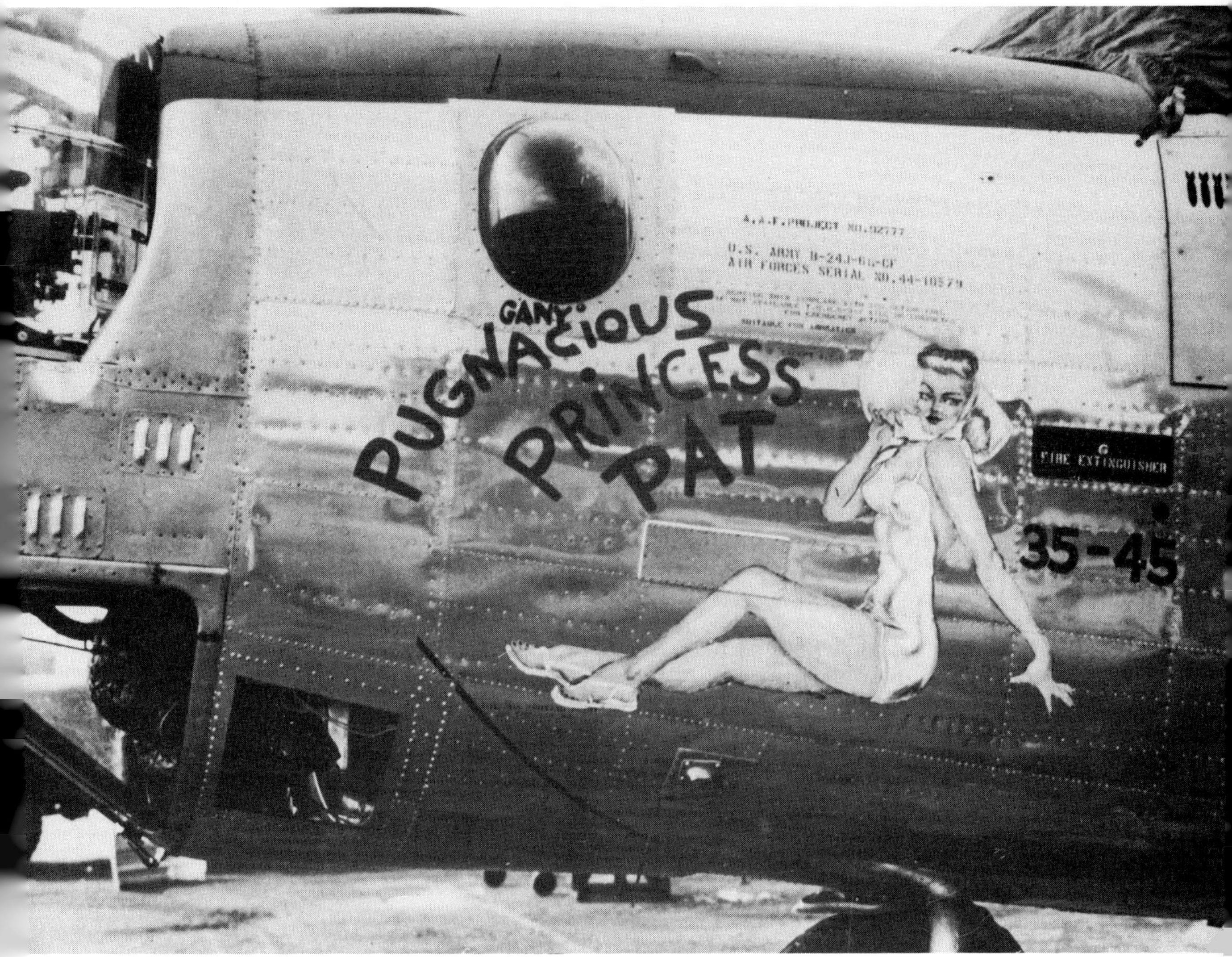
PUGNACIOUS
PRINCESS
PAT
FIRE EXTINGUISHER
35-45

83▼

WINNIE
FRANK
JOE

84▼

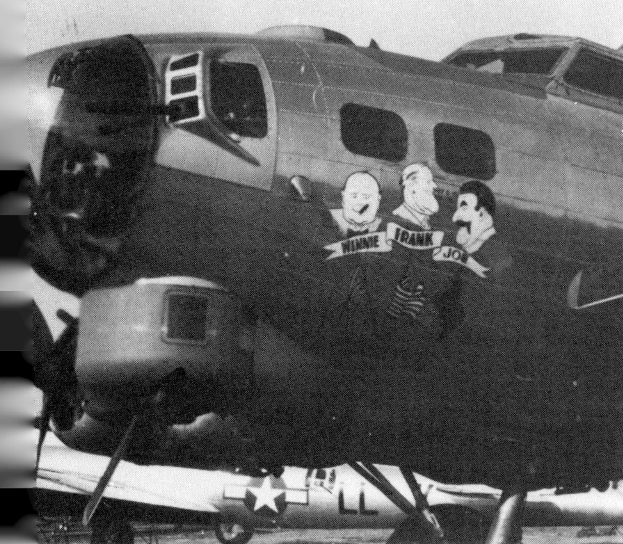

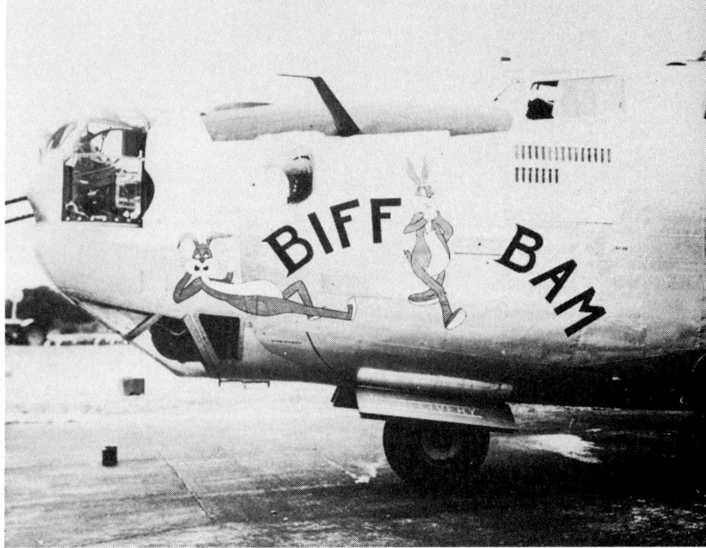

BIFF
BAM

The *Fotofax* series

A new range of pictorial studies of military subjects for the modeller, historian and enthusiast. Each title features a carefully-selected set of photographs plus a data section of facts and figures on the topic covered. With line drawings and detailed captioning, every volume represents a succinct and valuable study of the subject. New and forthcoming titles:

Warbirds
F-111 Aardvark
P-47 Thunderbolt
B-52 Stratofortress
Stuka!
Jaguar
US Strategic Air Power: Europe 1942–1945
Dornier Bombers
RAF in Germany

Vintage Aircraft
German Naval Air Service
Sopwith Camel
Fleet Air Arm, 1920–1939
German Bombers of WWI

Soldiers
World War One: 1914
World War One: 1915
World War One: 1916
Union Forces of the American Civil War
Confederate Forces of the American Civil War
Luftwaffe Uniforms
British Battledress 1945–1967 (2 vols)

Warships
Japanese Battleships, 1897–1945
Escort Carriers of World War Two
German Battleships, 1897–1945
Soviet Navy at War, 1941–1945
US Navy in World War Two, 1943–1944
US Navy, 1946–1980 (2 vols)
British Submarines of World War One

Military Vehicles
The Chieftain Tank
Soviet Mechanized Firepower Today
British Armoured Cars since 1945
NATO Armoured Fighting Vehicles
The Road to Berlin
NATO Support Vehicles

The *Illustrated* series

The internationally successful range of photo albums devoted to current, recent and historic topics, compiled by leading authors and representing the best means of obtaining your own photo archive.

Warbirds
US Spyplanes
USAF Today
Strategic Bombers, 1945–1985
Air War over Germany
Mirage
US Naval and Marine Aircraft Today
USAAF in World War Two
B-17 Flying Fortress
Tornado
Junkers Bombers of World War Two
Argentine Air Forces in the Falklands Conflict
F-4 Phantom Vol II
Army Gunships in Vietnam
Soviet Air Power Today
F-105 Thunderchief
Fifty Classic Warbirds
Canberra and B-57
German Jets of World War Two

Vintage Warbirds
The Royal Flying Corps in World War One
German Army Air Service in World War One
RAF between the Wars
The Bristol Fighter
Fokker Fighters of World War One
Air War over Britain, 1914–1918
Nieuport Aircraft of World War One

Tanks
Israeli Tanks and Combat Vehicles
Operation Barbarossa
Afrika Korps
Self-Propelled Howitzers
British Army Combat Vehicles 1945 to the Present
The Churchill Tank
US Mechanized Firepower Today
Hitler's Panzers
Panzer Armee Afrika
US Marine Tanks in World War Two

Warships
The Royal Navy in 1980s
The US Navy Today
NATO Navies of the 1980s
British Destroyers in World War Two
Nuclear Powered Submarines
Soviet Navy Today
British Destroyers in World War One
The World's Aircraft Carriers, 1914–1945
The Russian Convoys, 1941–1945
The US Navy in World War Two
British Submarines in World War Two
British Cruisers in World War One
U-Boats of World War Two
Malta Convoys, 1940–1943

Uniforms
US Special Forces of World War Two
US Special Forces 1945 to the Present
The British Army in Northern Ireland
Israeli Defence Forces, 1948 to the Present
British Special Forces, 1945 to Present
US Army Uniforms Europe, 1944–1945
The French Foreign Legion
Modern American Soldier
Israeli Elite Units
US Airborne Forces of World War Two
The Boer War
The Commandos World War Two to the Present
Victorian Colonial Wars

A catalogue listing these series and other Arms & Armour Press titles is available on request from: Sales Department, Arms & Armour Press, Artillery House, Artillery Row, London SW1P 1RT.